Lilo's Briefcase

Sneka C. Mohan

BookLeaf Publishing

India | USA | UK

Dearest,
Most people may have life harder than you
And that's never a key for invalidation
I hear you, we hear you.

Acknowledgement

I am who I am, thanks to every one of you who played your part to perfection: to my mother, for allowing me to become this strong version of self; to my father, for everything; to my baby brothers, for making life easier; to my family, for showing life in its truest of colours; to my best of friends, who are absolute firecrackers; to my brilliant inspirations; and to you, my fierce and loving self.

Preface

Meet Lilo. This 22-year-old woman woke up one day, decided to let things go, and was ready to heal–from the wounds others had left on her, from the hurt she'd inflicted upon herself, and from the exhaustion life had brought her. Next thing she knew, she was standing in front of the neighbourhood stationery store. "Bro, some letter covers please!" was her request, followed by a sheepish, "Something aesthetic". "Why letter covers?" you may ask. I don't know the answer either. I guess anxiety attacks have a prescription for scribbling.

First letter was easy-peasy-lemon-sqeezy. Done, dusted (Oh! Here comes the briefcase—more like a pouch. Don't tell her I said that.) and stored away in the trunk. Weeks passed by, then months, and years. 9 new letters added to the briefcase with 99 problems in queue. Arguably, our woman overestimated life and got her lessons. And when life went sideways for a while, her briefcase gained ash.

But Lilo never gave up on hope. The hope that someday the Sun will rise in the East and the world will work in her favour. The hope kept her filling up the briefcase with the magics of life, grateful relationships, and powerful dreams. I hope we travel through her letters to understand Lilo and you, me and everyone else on the journey.

Wise Man

David Siegel once said to me—
"You gotta let the ghosts go, Kid."
If I ever want to be the person I need to be.

It's time.

Shame

Some days, I can't accept it—
I was too young to understand,
but I knew, didn't I?

Wonder Woman

I marvel at her resilience,
facing the collapse of her world with courage.
She pressed on through violence and betrayal,
and though I can't fully understand—
the weight she carried,
I know it was immense.

The Manual

You left,
He left,
And she wept.

You took her dancing,
He had her dreaming,
And she is screaming.

You bought her betrayal,
He played her emotions,
When she asked for games.

Now the iron gates rattle,
Stopping anyone who wishes,
Crashing and crying,
Shouting and shaking,
Begging and bargaining.

"Where do I find the manual?" she fears,
To heal and erase the decade-old destruction,
To believe and build the broken bridge,
To keep no leg outside,
To forget and forgive.

"Do you know what's the saddest part?" she sighs,
Standing strong,
Knowing rights,
Preaching do's,
Fighting darks,
And failing all.

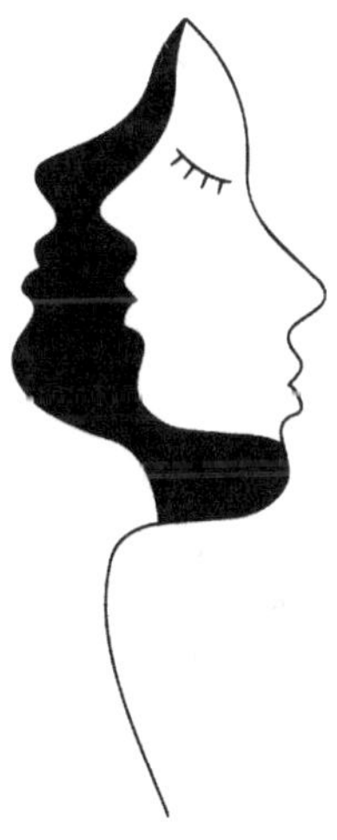

Pull

I am nothing but the sands
ready to be stolen back by the waves
under the blue moon
into the depths of the unknown, I feel home
sinking into the abyss
looking for magic and healing

Lost

Where did the beans spill?
I didn't notice the cracks.

When the shell of my mind and body felt too light,
All of my "is" became "was" and "were",
Was brilliant, *was* curious,
Was trustful, *was* loving,
Was happy, *was* healthy,
The only left *is*—lost.

When did the beans spill?
I didn't notice the cracks.

At 8? The world was confusing.
At 10? The pandora's box was shattering.
At 17? The dream was fading.
At 21? The heart was breaking.
At 26? The fog was thickening,
And getting lost became the new black.

Tattoo

I was 8 when I learned what fear of loss felt like.
It wasn't a big moment.
Just a simple explanation of blood pressure.
But it crushed me.
My heart felt like it was being squeezed from the
inside,
like clay I'd squish in my hands.
The sobbing wouldn't stop.
I clung to your shoulders, holding on too tight.
You said, *That's not going to happen.*
You said, *I'm not going anywhere.*
I kept those words. I needed them.

Then I was ten, and the pain got worse,
so sharp and sudden, it stole everything.
I shut a door that day,
threw the key somewhere I can't remember.
I begged everything you believed in.
Every god you prayed to.
I bargained with the air around me.
But no one listened.
When the begging ran dry,
I stopped feeling.
Or maybe, I just stopped trying to.
Yet still, it never really went away.
The pain just settled in,
stayed like some permanent ache,
and I went on—hoping, dreaming.

For a while, those stories were enough.
But they started fading too.
Now, the dreams don't visit.
Acceptance became this silent strength,
hushed cries on random Thursdays.

Then came these thoughts—
uninvited, unhealed.
A scene plays out—
another goodbye, another face.
My mind draws out—
funeral after funeral,
friends, family, everyone I've ever loved,
these endless scenes that show up
whenever they please.
No preparation helps.
I feel it all,
again, and again.
My mind just won't let go.
It's almost two decades now, and it's still alive.
Hollow but there, like it's part of me.
My heart hasn't stopped bracing for that next blow.

But every once in a while,
there's this hint, a whisper—maybe one day,
this heart will find a way to hold on—
without breaking.

Last Palette

I drew and drew and drew,
Hoping wildly that you'd come to me.
Through these ashen canvases,
Tearing and blazing like an inferno.

I drew and drew and drew,
Until the den reeked of oil.
I drew and drew and drew,
Wanting to feel our reds and golds.

I drew and drew and drew,
Whispering breathless pleas.
I drew and drew and drew,
Until you found me in whites.

Unclaimed Summer

I desired
I prayed

Oh my summer shower
You were everything I wanted
And everything beyond
You were the waves I never caught
And the dreams I never forgot

Oh my summer star
In the nooks of my books
Under the bridges of my hooks
You became the highlight of my nightmares

Oh my summer storm
You wrecked my whole city last night
Just to give her the sunshine the next day

She existed
She won

The Almost Brilliant

There was a time—
I shone, didn't I?
The questions came easy,
answers leapt like sparks,
and I felt them bend
to the shape of my mind.

But then I grew,
and the world spun faster—
where every voice spoke louder,
sharper, than mine.

I used to think I'd be someone
that the world would stop for.
Now, I slip by, unseen,
just a little better than most
but nowhere near enough—
just a small note in a song
I thought I'd sing alone.

I'm trying, always trying,
but the world only remembers the stars,
and I am just part of the sky,
caught in the quiet between dreams and dusk.

Still, a quiet hope waits,
lingers in me—
that somewhere inside this haze,
I'll find the piece I misplaced
and step back into the light
not blinding, but mine.

13

Cyclical

Sometimes I close my eyes shut,
Sometimes I pass by the street,
Sometimes I scroll past the world,
Sometimes I wish to save myself,
Many times I fail,
Every time I fall,
All the time I bleed.

P.O.P

Let me save myself.
Let me find love before heart shatters irreversibly.
Let me find peace with failure.
Let me whisper prayers of peace.

Tell me everything.
Tell me everything I know,
So I can heal myself.

Hold me tight,
So tight that I feel blood rushing into my brain.
So tight that I feel sleepy in your arms.
So tight that I heal.

Life Lately

Life lately is Melancholy.
Walking through loneliness
Feeling quadriplegic on Wednesdays
Zeroing into the voids of progress
Dating back to December

Life lately is a Mystery.
Walking into a white tunnel
Feeling a sense of curiosity
Zeroing in on the hope tattooed
Dating a fantasyland

Life lately is a Miracle.
When the essence of the ocean
Erases the pain and despair
Between the layovers and laptops—
Grateful for sunburns over heartbreaks

Life lately is Magical.
When the escape from reality
Eases the mind and soul
Between bending water and breathing fire—
Grateful for dragons over avatars

The Long Run

I dream in fragments—
each one a star I've caught
and lost again,
like a night sky with too many constellations
to trace with tired eyes.

The world keeps asking,
Why haven't you crossed that line yet?
But they don't know
how long I've been running on empty,
how many mornings I've woken
to find my hands too weak
to hold the weight of what I thought
I could do.

Some days, time slips away—
a river I can't swim fast enough.
and I watch my plans drift by,
wondering if I'll ever catch them,
or if I'm already too late.

But I know this:
as long as my heart holds those dreams,
they're alive, waiting,
ready to rise with me,
when the moment is right.

The road is long—
but so am I.

So if you think I'm just talking,
just waiting,
just dreaming—
know this:

I am moving.

And nothing,
not time,
not doubt,
not even you,
can take my dreams away.

Kiss of Magic

Sometimes all I need is—
a whisper of stardust and alchemy's touch
In the depth of despair, where sorrows clutch
I hope for light, a smile, a gentle brush

#DYKHMILY

I count myself lucky—
eleven years, eleven hearts,
or maybe more.
Women who made life easier
without even trying.

You taught me
how to share a room,
and that girls' schools
are the most fun anyone could ever have.

We forced each other to stay awake
in study rooms,
but it was the Saturday movie nights—
crowded lawn, old projectors,
everyone laughing or crying at the same scene—
that reminded me
how much I loved stories.

In college, I learned
that soulmates don't always wear rings—
sometimes, they braid your hair
or tell you it's okay to cry,
then make you laugh
so hard you forget why you started.

Like a twin pea in your pod,
a voice saying,
"I'll always have your back."

Some of you taught me
that bunking classes
for the canteen's samosas
is the only core memory
worth keeping.

I remember makeshift birthday cakes,
biscuits stacked high with creativity,
fights in bathroom queues
that turned into jokes we'd retell for years.
We cursed the mess food daily,
but somehow, those meals gave us
the loudest laughter of our lives.

We promised to be on time for class,
then bunked the same lectures.
We vowed to top exams,
but it was the "no arrears" celebrations
that mattered most.

From being the loudest,
to sharing those innocent yet dirty
telepathic jokes
only we could understand—
we became a language of our own.

People say real friends stick through everything—
but we knew better.
Life pulls us in different directions.
Sometimes, all you get
is one season—
one year of laughter,
one weekend of tears.
But if it's real,
if it's honest,
if it's full of love,
that's enough.

Every phase of my life,
I had you—
gorgeous, devilishly brilliant women.

Did I ever tell you how much I love you?
Did you ever realize how much I always will?

Chef's Table: Adulthood

a handful of late-night talks
spilled across empty streets,

and two cups of laughter
from friends who stay,

a dash of doubt
(it keeps things honest),

one spoonful of first love
and a pinch of letting go.

stir in vulnerability – raw and real,
and a heaping scoop of ambition
(always rising, never enough).

add a sprinkle of YOLO!
for flavor,

a dash of impulse decisions
that might burn, but who's counting,

and a handful of dark circles
as proof, you've been living.

mix in heartbreak,
not too much, but enough to remember,

and a spoonful of humor,
to keep things from getting heavy.

add mistakes—the good kind,
and the kind that stings a bit,

a cup of quiet dreams kept close,
and hope, as much as you can find.

fold in empathy, finely chopped,
a taste that lingers, and deepens with time.

sprinkle in strands of gray hair,
drop in tears when they come
(you'll know when they're needed),

and finish with moments of courage—
small, but fierce,

all served with a side of *"I'll be fine."*

Serve as is:
unfinished, unfolding,
meant to be tasted
slowly.

Soulmate

If Soulmate is my book
You would be my preface
Everything I need
Everything I don't have

Echo

You were my red and green
I let you go
I looked for a white
And hoped for a green

I let us go
Like you said so
I let us go

Then why do you claw
I let you go,
only to find my red *again*

Utopian Prince

My castle didn't crumble overnight.
I took my sweet time out.
When the cracks appeared,
I hoped the walls would stand.

With easy escapes and poor excuses,
every night was a battle.
Flight or fight was never a question
until the prince smiled.

He was the dream
every princess would pray for—
A light of love and kindness.
And he became the ruler in mine.
Yet by my hand, he was lost to me,
and though the ache runs deep—
it's a wound I chose.

Every time I reached for him,
with a touch that promises everything,
I felt my hand pulling back,
caught in a web of uncertainty I couldn't untangle.
And though I tried to hide it,
my heart echoed the same,
a silent answer.

I stood in a pattern I couldn't escape,
one I saw so clearly —
the hurt, the distance, my cold steps
repeating, like echoes through stone halls.

My castle didn't crumble overnight
I slammed the door so hard
that the walls fell
and when the chariot left
with him, the kindest soul,
Everything & Everywhere hurt.

He deserved more than a flickering love,
waiting for warmth that often vanished.
And while it broke me to let him go,
I couldn't let my loyalty wear him thin,
waiting for a promise
that was already ashen.

My castle didn't crumble overnight.
I took my sweet time unraveling the fortress,
carrying the weight of his kindness,
calling out to the universe—
a love that stands solid,
a warmth that holds unbroken.

Is it selfish?

How is it selfish of me?
To wish that you'd fight for me.
How is it selfish of me?
To wish that you'd meant the words.

How is it not selfish of you?
To act like I don't get hurt.
How is it not selfish of you?
To act like I didn't matter.

How is it selfish of me?
To choose myself.
How is it selfish of me?
To choose your wellbeing.

How is it not selfish of others?
To say I am unreasonable.
How is it not selfish of others?
To say I am hypocritical.

When all I ever asked was for—
someone to fight for me.

What Ocean Did

The waves rolled in, soft and steady,
then rose to a roar that filled the shore,
a susurration, low and endless,
like it knew every secret I'd ever held.

The swash of waves washed over my feet,
I stood there, listening to the backwash
pulling back secrets, laying them bare,
letting go of all that hurt, then pulling me in.

It was just waves, water, and sky,
but it felt like the ocean knew my name,
in its steady crash, I heard it say:
Let go.
and in its depths, I found a quiet answer—
to trust the calm, to trust the storm.

Acoustics

Life has many significant acoustics—
in the rustle of leaves,
in the sounds of waves crashing,
when a shower becomes a thunderstorm,
with the white noise of the bedroom,
in the wails of life-hood,
from the breaths of a lover,
in the hush before a kiss,
when dining is set,
with the flicker of candlelight in the stillness,
in the laughter and sighs,
with the sound of rain tapping on the roof,
urging you to live—
vicariously, beautifully, and wholeheartedly.

It's Over

I realised I am over it,
when my pen refused to bleed your name,
and my uke played a G major.

December's Shift

December
Was first love and remembrance,
Was betrayal and relief,
Was friendship and solitude,
Was magical and miraculous,
Was detox and de-stress,
Was Purple, Blue, and Grey.

December
had always been hard,
Then it became harder.
But when you arrived—
the new sun in my orbit,
crushing my demons with heat waves,
cuddling my inner child with warmth,
cooling my rage with ice,
neither 4 nor 14 hurts.

You, Unwritten

"What's your love language?" a sign read.
You are.

You are my stained glass window,
Messy, beautiful, and vibrant.

I pause my world to watch you talk
Background blurs—
Everything else, an NPC.

Every smile I reciprocate
With hearts in my eyes,
Fireworks in my mind,
Butterflies in my chest.

I found the prettiest soul,
The kindest heart,
The fiercest passion.

You are my medley—
Short-lived adrenaline, and—
When memories fade,
You'll be the intuition I believe.

#AFBF

I wonder who I would've been
if not for you—
a wordless specimen.

Have you ever thought
how, on a midday afternoon,
life flips 180—
and you wonder
who you were the day before?
or a month? a decade?

When the world was masqueraded,
caught between the struggles of
staying alive and being alive,
spiraling down felt the easiest.

A little carousel of pictures, videos—
and it was love at first sight
for genuineness,
mindfulness,
kindness.

And the words rang in my head—
"I want what they have."

When the truths of—
when you need it the most hit me
I was already healing.

From the monotony
society calls survival,
From the emotional ambiguities
that felt world-ending
From the betrayal and heartbreaks
that rewired everything.

I wonder who I would've been
if not for you—
A child boxed in by betrayal?
A youngster trying to fit into one?

I will never know.
Being unaware never felt so free.
And the words keep flowing.

Continuance

Every day I wake up,
trying to restart my life,
hoping one day I'll become,
the self I am proud of.

Each time I try to reset,
I fail miserably,
but still, I hope that one day,
it will all pay off.

I may be battling a hidden villain,
yet the person I want to be—
the one my family would be proud of,
the one my father would be proud of—
is still a work in progress.

Every time I pull myself up,
every time I choose to try again,
every time I hope for a miracle,
I tell myself that someday I'll breathe,
the way I want to,
in a way that fills me with pride.

I just want to be proud of myself,
to have achieved my dreams, and my ambitions.
At the end of the day, that's what matters:

I am what matters.
My choice to try again is what matters,
even if failure is all I get,
even when others stop believing in me.

Sunday, a race day

In the race against doubt,
I take my place at the pole,
engine roaring, heart revving,
feeling the heat, the thrill,
adrenaline pulsing through my veins.

Lap by lap, I lean into each chicane,
every twist—a test,
but I know my pace,
not the speed others dictate,
I slipstream when I need rest,
until it's time to pull ahead.

I accelerate, throttle open,
leaning into the apex of my own drive,
where confidence rises
in the roar of my engine—
not loud, but steady.

Pit stops— my chance to breathe,
to refuel, recharge, let my crew—
fix the cracks, remind me of who I am.

Telemetry speaks,
a race engineer in my mind—
monitoring my heart & will,
keeping me steady & in control,
as I'm pushed to the limit.

But the grid is tight, competition wheel-to-wheel,
yellow flag warns me, downforce grounds me
as I surge past grid penalties,
those mistakes that teach me to be strong.

And as I cross the line,
I know that pole position was never about speed,
it was the courage to start,
to roar louder than my fear,
to be both throttle and brake,

I know I am my own constructor, my own engine,
built not just to endure, but to drive my life
on my own terms.

Rainy Days

Most days—
Be the sprinkle,
That makes people dance.
Be the rain shower,
That cools down the earth.
Be the drizzle,
That brings romance into the air.
Be the veil,
That breathes life into the beings.

Some days—
Be the cloudburst,
That brings an electrifying presence.
Be the thunderstorm,
That adds drama to the show.
Be the deluge,
That shows unrelenting power.

On all days—
Be the cyclone,
That reshapes lives.
Be the typhoon,
That commands resilience.

One day—
Be the Tsunami,
A rare, unforgettable force—
That leaves a lasting change.

D-DAY

Chaos lingers still,
yet tomorrow softly hums—
I am worth the wait.